Earthlings

Inside and Out

A Space Alien Studies the Human Body

Written By Valerie Wyatt

Illustrated By Dušan Petričić

Kids Can Press

For Larry

Acknowledgments

A book is always a joint project of many people. My thanks go to Dr. James Dickson for checking the manuscript. His impressive anatomical knowledge and generous sharing of his expertise were much appreciated. Thanks also to Drs Marjon Blouw and Margaret Basher for checking illustrations and text midway through the process and to Dr. Rob Koopmans for helping with last-minute questions. Any errors that may have crept in are my responsibility solely.

At Kids Can Press, I would like to thank Marie Bartholomew for her good humor and creativity as the book evolved; Dušan Petričić for his whimsical and charming illustrations; and Charis Wahl for her amazing editorial expertise — and for inventing Danoid. Thanks always to Ricky Englander and Valerie Hussey for taking care of all the other parts of the publishing process. Finally, my thanks to Liz MacLeod for her support and suggestions.

Kids Can Press acknowledges the financial support of the Ontario Arts Council, the Canada Council for the Arts and the Department of Cultural Heritage.

Published in Canada by
Kids Can Press Ltd.
29 Birch Avenue
Toronto, ON M4V 1E2

Published in the U.S. by
Kids Can Press Ltd.
85 River Rock Drive, Suite 202
Buffalo, NY 14207

Edited by Charis Wahl
Designed by Marie Bartholomew
Printed in Hong Kong by Book Art Inc., Toronto

CM 99 0 9 8 7 6 5 4 3 2 1
PA 99 0 9 8 7 6 5 4 3 2 1

Canadian Cataloguing in Publication Data
Wyatt, Valerie
        Earthlings inside and out

Includes index.
ISBN 1-55074-511-5 (bound)   ISBN 1-55074-513-1 (pbk.)

1. Human physiology – Juvenile literature.   2. Human anatomy – Juvenile literature.
Body, Human – Juvenile literature.   I. Petričić, Dušan.   II. Title.

QP37.W92 1999   j612   C98-932897-X

contents

First encounter

Earlier this year a spacecraft from Planet Memo veered off course while passing through an interstellar dust cloud. When the dust cleared, the pilot, a Memoid named Danoid, spotted a strange blue planet. Danoid steered the spacecraft close to the planet's surface and beamed these scans back to Central Command.

"Request permission to study the alien life-forms, Commander."

"Permission granted, Danoid. The planet is called Earth. You will find all known information about it in EARTHDATABANK. Report regularly on your findings."

"Roger and out, Commander."

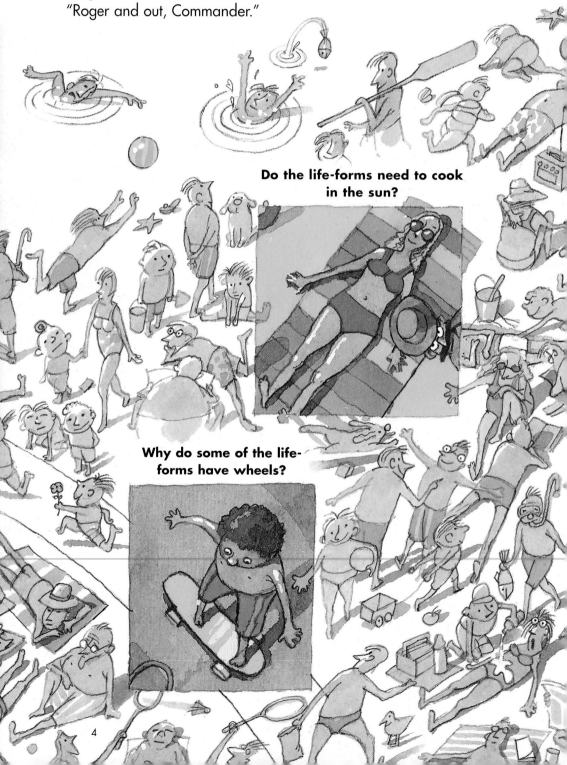

Do the life-forms need to cook in the sun?

Why do some of the life-forms have wheels?

Refueling?

Several species at a feeding ground?

Possible subject for further study?

Pete meets Danoid

"Hey, cool."

The thing was sitting behind the fish-and-chip stand on the boardwalk. It was shiny and red and had more buttons than a VCR. Pete reached out to push a button.

A polite machine voice said, "Please do not touch."

Just like a talking car alarm, thought Pete.

"Not a talking car alarm," said the voice. "A Danoid."

Pete jumped back. Yow! This thing could read minds! The hairs on the back of his neck stood on end.

"Danoid from Planet Memo," the machine voice continued.

Yeah, right, thought Pete. And I'm Pinocchio.

"Nice to meet you, Pinocchio," said the alien. Its binocularlike eyeballs popped out of its head and waved. Pete didn't bother correcting it.

"Danoid wishes to study an Earthling body." The thing's eyeballs were peering at Pete from different angles.

"No way!"

There was a long pause. Then the machine voice said, "Cooperate and you can ride in Danoid's spacecraft."

Pete knew better than to get into a stranger's car. But no one had said anything about an alien spacecraft. Besides, he had a science fair project on the human body due in two weeks. Maybe the alien had some brilliant ideas.

Pete took a deep breath, looked around to make sure no one saw him talking to an alien, and finally said, "Deal."

The Earthling

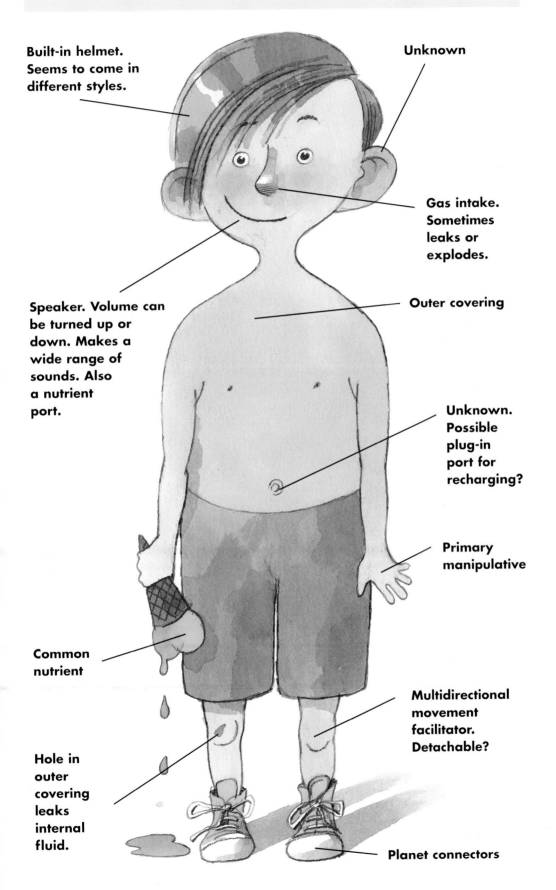

Built-in helmet. Seems to come in different styles.

Unknown

Gas intake. Sometimes leaks or explodes.

Speaker. Volume can be turned up or down. Makes a wide range of sounds. Also a nutrient port.

Outer covering

Unknown. Possible plug-in port for recharging?

Primary manipulative

Common nutrient

Multidirectional movement facilitator. Detachable?

Hole in outer covering leaks internal fluid.

Planet connectors

Danoid gets under Pete's skin

"Preparing to scan the Earthling's exterior," said the voice. And with that, Danoid's eyeballs zeroed in on Pete's arm.

Pete flinched. "Is this going to hurt?"

"Negative." The eyeballs started to glow and move. Pete could feel a slight tingling, but no pain.

A picture appeared on Danoid's shiny surface.

Earthling skin

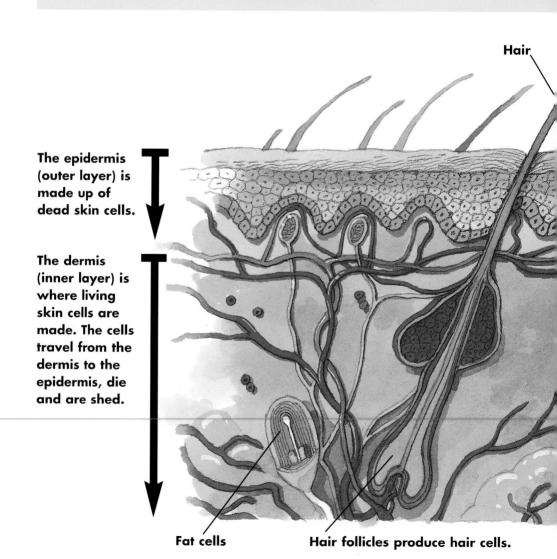

Hair

The epidermis (outer layer) is made up of dead skin cells.

The dermis (inner layer) is where living skin cells are made. The cells travel from the dermis to the epidermis, die and are shed.

Fat cells

Hair follicles produce hair cells.

"Hey!" Pete peered at the picture. "That's my skin. Gross."

"What is skin?"

"My, uh, external covering." The picture faded and Danoid's metallic surface shimmered in the sunlight.

Pete thought about touching it, then chickened out. "What's *your* skin made of?"

"Druconium."

"Dru *who*?" asked Pete.

"Druconium. 'Combining the toughness of kryptonite with the rich finish of an Astroblaster.' That was what the sales unit said when Danoid bought it."

"You *bought* your skin?"

"Affirmative. Where did yours come from?"

"I've had it since I was born ... er, made."

Danoid's eyeballs popped out. "Not possible. It still fits you."

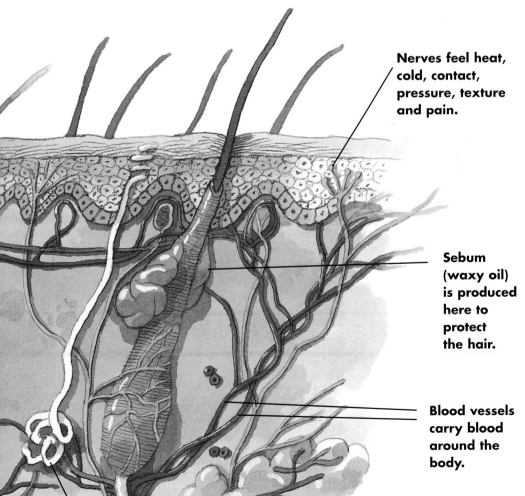

Nerves feel heat, cold, contact, pressure, texture and pain.

Sebum (waxy oil) is produced here to protect the hair.

Blood vessels carry blood around the body.

Sweat glands produce liquid to cool the body.

"It grew with me."

Danoid whirred and clicked. "Data does not compute."
The alien made a sound like popcorn popping, then announced,
"This is Danoid's fourth covering since becoming operational. The first two
became too small. The third was dented by a meteorite."

"Human skin can grow and repair itself," Pete said proudly. "It's alive."

Danoid's eyeballs quivered. "A covering that is alive?"

Pete showed Danoid the cut on his knee. "See this? In a week or two, my
skin will be good as new."

"Where is your repair kit?"

"It's built in. A clot of blood plugs the hole and stops the bleeding. The clot
gets hard — we call it a scab — and stays until the skin underneath is
repaired." Pete knew a lot about scabs. He had planned to do his science
fair project on them, until his father had accidentally vacuumed up his scab
collection.

"Danoid will investigate skin repair." The eyeballs floated over the cut.
Three pictures popped up on the alien's shiny surface.

Earthling skin repair

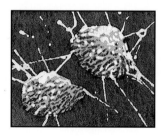
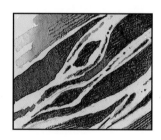

Mast cells make the area hot, sore and red. The heat speeds up the repairs. The soreness reminds the Earthling to be careful while the injury is healing.

Phagocytes are "cleaner" cells. They eat dead bacteria around the wound.

Fibroblasts are "weaver" cells. They knit the skin together.

Danoid turned slightly green and made a sound like a burp. Big trouble. Was the alien about to be sick? Time for a distraction. Pete held out his fingers. "Check out *this* skin."

It worked. Danoid's coloring was returning to what seemed normal for an alien.

"What are the ridges for?" asked Danoid.

"To get a better grip. Hey! Maybe that can be my science project. Testing the gripping power of different finger coverings."

A gripping experiment

Equipment

10 flat toothpicks
a watch or clock that shows seconds
a pencil and paper
clear tape
masking tape
different kinds of gloves (rubber, wool, etc.)

Method

1. Spread the toothpicks out on a table.
2. With one hand, try to pick up the toothpicks one at a time. How many can you pick up in five seconds? Write down the number.
3. Use clear tape to cover the fingertips of your gripping hand. Now how many toothpicks can you pick up in five seconds? Record the number.

4. Test the masking tape and then the gloves in the same way, and record the number of toothpicks picked up with each. Which worked best? Bare fingers or one of the coverings?

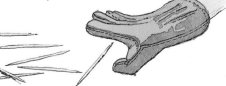

EARTHDATABANK: Skin

The average Earthling skin measures about 2 m² (more than 22 sq. ft.) and weighs about 2.5 kg (5 1/2 lb.).

The Earthling continually sheds dead skin. By age 70, the average Earthling has lost 48 kg (106 lb.) of skin.

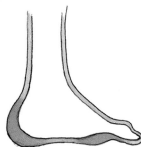

Earthling skin is thin in some places and thick in others. The tough skin that covers the heels of feet and the palms of hands is the thickest, to withstand wear and tear. The eyelid has the thinnest skin.

Pete felt something crawling in his hair. He reached up to swat it and hit one of Danoid's eyeballs.

"You were cruising my scalp!"

"Why do Earthlings have dead keratin growing out of their skin?" asked Danoid.

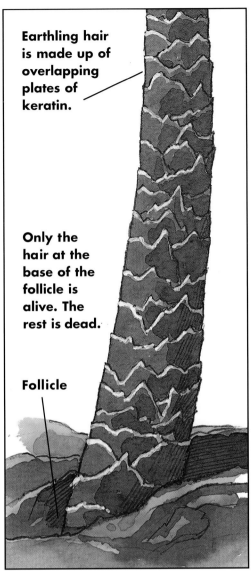

Earthling hair is made up of overlapping plates of keratin.

Only the hair at the base of the follicle is alive. The rest is dead.

Follicle

Earthling hair

"You mean hair?" Pete wasn't used to thinking of his hair as keratin. Or dead. He shrugged. Then he remembered a caveman movie he'd just seen. "I think people once had lots of hair all over to keep them warm. Like built-in clothes."

Danoid's eyeballs scanned Pete's shorts. "Now Earthlings have clothes. Why do you also need hair?"

Pete thought of how much he hated haircuts and the sting of shampoo in his eyes. "Good question." But Danoid had already moved on — to Pete's fingernails.

"These are hard, like druconium," the alien announced.

"Yeah, but they're alive. They grow all the time."

"How fast?"

"Another good question."

How fast do fingernails grow?

Equipment

nail polish

Do all fingernails grow at the same speed? What about toenails? Do some people's nails grow faster than others?

Method

1. Paint a line of nail polish along the base of one fingernail.

2. After one week, measure how far the line has moved from the base of the fingernail.

3. Measure after two weeks, then three weeks and four weeks. Repaint the line if it starts to chip off. How much does a fingernail grow in a month?

EARTHDATABANK: Hair

Earthlings lose 50 to 80 hairs a day. New hairs grow to take their place — on most people.

The number of hairs an Earthling has on its head depends on hair color. Blonds have about 140 000 hairs, redheads about 90 000, and Earthlings with black or brown hair have about 110 000 hairs.

Hairs grow about 1 cm (3/8 in.) a month.

Hair is curly or straight depending on the shape of the hair follicle out of which it grows. Straight hair grows out of a round follicle. Curly hair grows from an oval or flat follicle.

Every part of the Earthling body, except the palms of hands and the soles of feet, has hair.

Fingernails and toenails are made of the same material as hair: keratin.

Report to: The Commander
From: Danoid
Subject: The subject's exterior

Pinocchio's outer covering, called "skin," is less expensive and more durable than Memoid coverings — although not nearly as attractive. He does not need to purchase new coverings as he grows. His existing covering grows with him. Damaged or dead bits fall off and are replaced.

Skin seems to protect the subject's inner components from germs, injury and solar radiation. Nerves in the skin send information to a Central Processing Unit.

Wirelike "hairs" made of dead keratin protrude from the skin all over his body. The purpose of these hairs will require further study. Most of the hairs are clustered on the top of the head. Pinocchio reports that he must apply mixtures to these hairs and slice off their ends from time to time.

Danoid delves into Pete's brain

"Where is your CPU?"
"My what?" asked Pete.

"Your Central Processing Unit. The unit that runs your systems."
"Oh — you mean my brain." Pete pointed to his head. "It's in here."
"Remove it for viewing, please."
"My brain? Are you crazy?" Pete began to panic. "It's attached!"
"Then Danoid will scan the brain in place."
Pete felt a tickle in his nose as Danoid's eyeballs swirled over his head. Then this image appeared on Danoid's shiny surface.

Functions of the Earthling brain

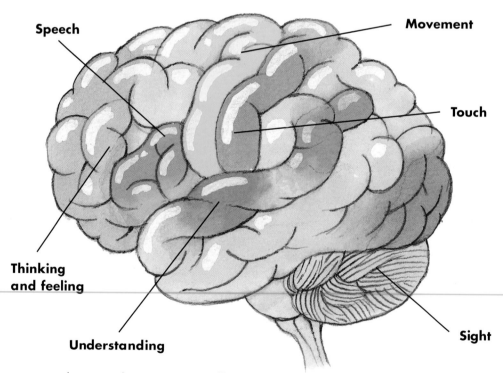

Speech

Movement

Touch

Thinking and feeling

Understanding

Sight

Danoid stopped scanning. "Different parts of the Earthling brain control different functions." Danoid rocked back and forth. "Zweird!"

Pete was just starting to relax when the alien spoke again. "Danoid will now scan inside the Earthling brain."

"Inside my brain? Wait a —" But before Pete could say another word, his nose tickle turned into a sneeze. And then things went out of control. First Pete wondered whether fish sleep, then he twirled on tiptoe, got sweaty palms and remembered the twelve-times table.

"Whoa!" he shouted. Then he had a brainstorm. "Scan the memory part again, okay? Maybe I can remember where I left my baseball cap."

The three main parts of the Earthling brain

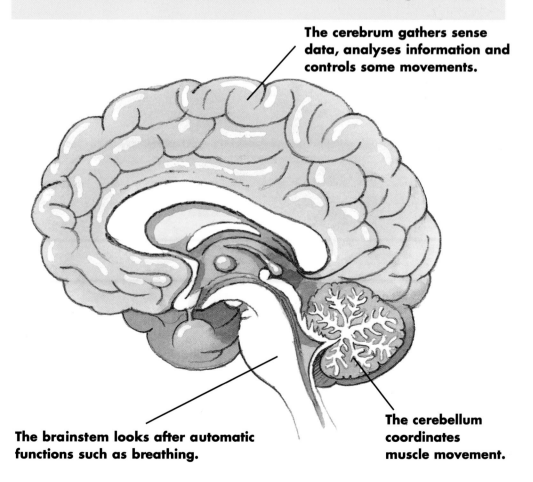

The cerebrum gathers sense data, analyses information and controls some movements.

The brainstem looks after automatic functions such as breathing.

The cerebellum coordinates muscle movement.

"According to EARTHDATABANK, the Earthling brain sends messages from one part of the brain to another at 400 km/h (250 m.p.h.)," said Danoid. "How fast do messages travel from the brain to the other parts of the body?"

A test of brain speed

Equipment

a ruler

Method

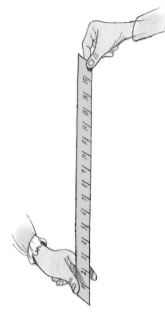

1. Hold a ruler vertically by the end that has the high numbers. Place the other end between someone's thumb and index finger. Her fingers should be at the 1-cm (or 1-in.) mark and about 2.5 cm (1 in.) apart.

2. Tell her to grab the ruler with her thumb and index finger when you drop it.

3. Drop the ruler without warning. Check where her fingers hold the ruler. The lower the number the faster the message traveled from her brain to her hand.

EARTHDATABANK: Brain

The Earthling brain looks like a giant walnut, weighs as much as a small cabbage and feels like soft jelly.

The weight of the brain is about 1/50 of an Earthling's total body weight.

The brain can store 100 trillion units of information over a lifetime.

Report to: The Commander
From: Danoid
Subject: The subject's Central Processing Unit

Pinocchio's CPU is called a "brain" and seems to be a data bank and operating program combined.

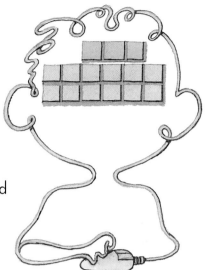

The data bank contains words and images that can be accessed as needed. Storage is called "memory." Accessing is called "learning" or "remembering." The subject's language is also drawn from the data bank.

The operating program runs nonstop. It controls muscles needed for the survival of the life-form (such as the heart muscles), as well as the essential systems of digestion and breathing. (Danoid will provide data on the heart, digestion and breathing in future reports.) The brain also operates muscles used for movement. Example: when Pinocchio wants to scratch an itch on his external covering, a message is sent to the brain from the location of the itch. The brain signals the hand to move to the site and scratch.

The brain also seems to control fear, happiness, anger and other Earthling "emotions," or TSMs (Temporary System Malfunctions), as we call them.

Danoid senses Pete's senses

A whiff of fries and vinegar tickled Pete's nose. "Mmmmm. Smell that," he said to Danoid.

"Explain 'smell,' please."

Never had Pete imagined he'd be standing at a fish-and-chip stand trying to describe smell to an alien. He grabbed a bottle of vinegar from the counter. "Where's your nose?" he asked. A hose snaked out from Danoid's side. "Not your hose," said Pete. "Your nose."

Danoid sounded embarrassed. "This model is not equipped with a nose."

"Then how do you know what things smell like?"

"Explain 'smell,' please."

This was going nowhere. Pete pointed to Danoid's eyeballs. "You can see me with those things, right?"

"Affirmative." The eyeballs separated and bobbled. "These are Danoid's data receptors."

"Data receptors? You mean you can also hear, taste, smell and touch with them?"

Danoid bounced up and down, but said nothing.

Pete tried again. He held out the bottle of vinegar. "How would you find out about what's in this bottle?"

Danoid wiggled the data receptors. "Danoid would conduct a scan to extract all available data."

Bingo! "That's what my senses do. They scan stuff and send the information to my brain." Pete pointed to his eyes and ears. "I see and hear with these." Then he pointed to his nose and mouth. "I smell and taste with these. And I feel things all over my body."

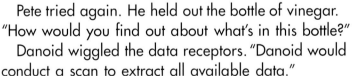

"Zweird dude," said Danoid. "Prepare to investigate Earthling senses."

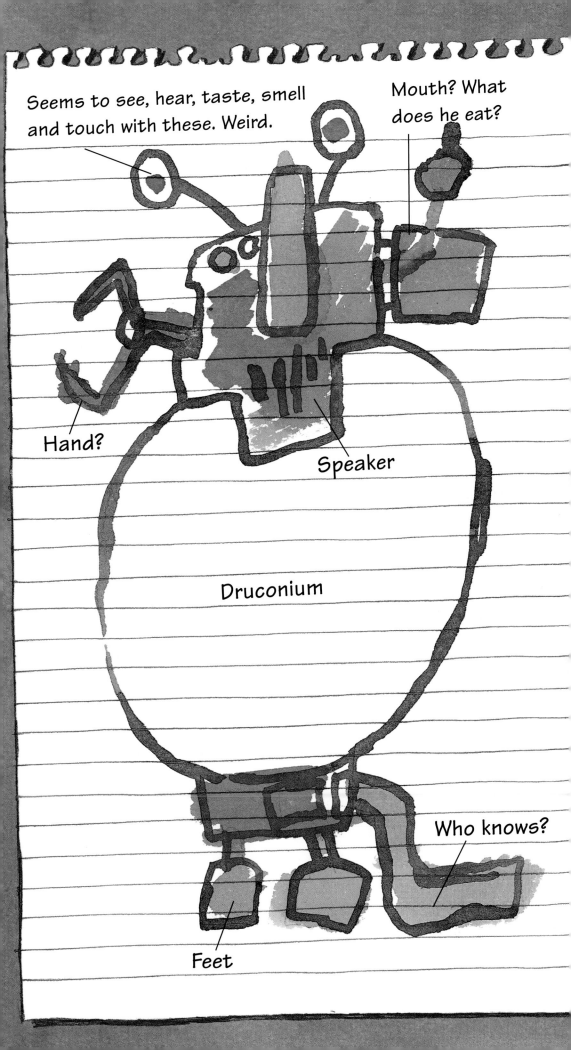

"EARTHDATABANK says the Earthling nose can detect 4000 different odors. Demonstrate please."

Demonstrate smelling? Then Pete had an idea. He splashed a bit more vinegar on Danoid's vinegary data receptor and squeezed a lemon wedge over the other. "Can you tell the difference?" he asked.

Both data receptors glowed. "Mild acid," said the machine voice, "and ... mild acid."

"Nope — vinegar and lemon. Check this out. I'll close my eyes and you put the lemon or the vinegar under my nose. I'll guess the smell."

Pete closed his eyes and sniffed. "Vinegar," he said. Suddenly he smelled lemon — Danoid must have switched. Then things went haywire. "Vinegar. Lemon. Vinegar. Lemon. Vin— I can't tell anymore!"

Can your sense of smell be fooled?

Equipment

6 smelly foods
(such as blue cheese, onion, lemon, vinegar, crushed garlic and soya sauce)
6 small jars with lids
a blindfold

Method

1. Put a different kind of food into each jar and close the lids.

2. Tie a blindfold on someone. One by one, open the jars and let him smell the contents. Close the lids after each sniff. How many smells can he identify before his sniffer gives out?

3. Repeat the test, opening the jars and letting him sniff the foods in different order. Does the order of the smells make a difference?

Does sense of smell fade as you get older? Test people of various ages to see.

Pete sniffed his fries, shook on some salt and popped a couple into his mouth. "Yum!"

"Yum?"

Pete held out the fries. "These taste greabbllechh!" Yikes! There was something furry on his tongue. A data receptor!

Pete tried to spit it out, but no luck. He tasted something bitter, then salty. As Danoid's data receptor moved across his tongue, he tasted apple pie with soya sauce, followed by fish with grape jelly. Then this picture appeared.

Earthling taste receptors

Bumps called papillae cover the tongue. They contain taste buds with long taste cells. Food mixed with saliva flows over the taste cells, which decode the taste and send a message to the brain.

Pittoowee! Pete spat out the receptor and wiped his mouth. That was gross!

"You do not taste good," said Danoid.

Pete was confused. Was Danoid saying that he tasted bad, or that his sense of taste was bad? Before he could ask, the alien's data receptors swirled over his nose.

"According to Danoid's analysis, without your sense of smell you could hardly taste at all."

"No way!" Then Pete remembered how tasteless everything seemed when he had a cold. That gave him an idea.

SCIENCE FAIR IDEA

How important is smell to the sense of taste?

Equipment

a glass each of cranberry juice, pineapple juice and apricot juice
a blindfold

Method

1. Find someone who is willing to do a juice taste test. Do not tell her what the juices are or let her see the three glasses — the color may give the juices away.

2. Tie the blindfold over your subject's eyes.

3. Ask her to plug her nose securely. Carefully put the glass of cranberry juice into her hand. Ask her to take a sip and tell you what flavor it is. Did she guess correctly?

4. Test your subject with the other two juices. She should have her nose plugged when she tastes them. How many correct guesses does she make?

5. Repeat the test. This time your subject should keep the blindfold on, but not plug her nose. How many correct guesses does she make? Does her sense of smell help her sense of taste?

Test other juices and solid foods too. Is it hard to taste all of them with your nose plugged, or just some?

"Danoid will now test the Earthling sense of hearing."

Pete sure hoped none of his friends walked by. How could he explain why he had an alien's data receptor in his ear?

The Earthling ear

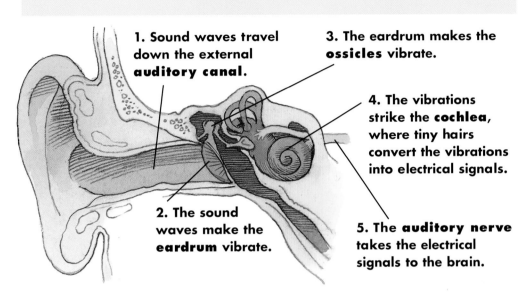

1. Sound waves travel down the external **auditory canal.**

2. The sound waves make the **eardrum** vibrate.

3. The eardrum makes the **ossicles** vibrate.

4. The vibrations strike the **cochlea,** where tiny hairs convert the vibrations into electrical signals.

5. The **auditory nerve** takes the electrical signals to the brain.

With a *Fwoop!* Danoid removed the data receptor from Pete's ear, and the picture faded. "Why do you have two ears?" asked Danoid.

SCIENCE FAIR IDEA

Can two ears hear better than one?

Equipment

a blindfold
2 paper clips
a pencil and paper

Method

1. Have someone sit in a chair in the middle of a room. Blindfold her.

2. Tap the two paper clips together while walking away, until she can barely hear the tapping.

3. From this distance, walk in a circle around her. In any order you wish, tap in front, behind, to the left and to the right of your subject. Can she tell where the tapping is coming from?

4. Now ask her to plug one ear with a finger, and try the same test again. Is it easier or harder for her to locate the source of the tapping?

Test other people. Do people hear as well with one ear as with two?

Pete was definitely seeing things — bright green things. Danoid must be testing his sense of sight.

The Earthling eye

1. Light enters the eye through the cornea, and passes through the pupil.

3. The lens bends the light so that it hits the retina at the back of the eye.

4. In the retina, receptors called "rods" register shape and movement, while "cones" register colors.

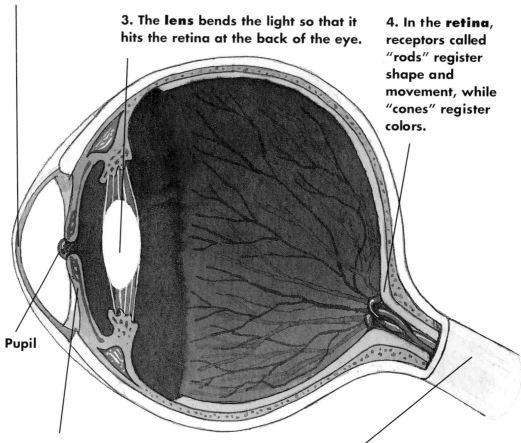

Pupil

2. The iris is made up of tiny muscles that adjust the size of the pupil and the amount of light allowed in.

5. All data is passed to the optic nerve, which takes it to the brain.

Suddenly the green glow vanished. Pete blinked.
"Why are your eyes on the front of your head?" asked Danoid.
What did Mrs. Whipple say about eyes? It was in science class and ... Pete scanned his memory bank. Got it! "All humans used to be hunters. Having eyes on the front of the head helped them judge distances. That was important because hunters had to shoot arrows and throw rocks at animals. I guess it worked so well, we just stuck with it."

Do two eyes help you judge distances?

Equipment

a jar
10 coins or buttons

Method

1. Sit at one end of a long table and have someone sit at the other. Put the jar in front of you. Hold a coin in one hand about 25 cm (10 in.) above the jar and off to one side.

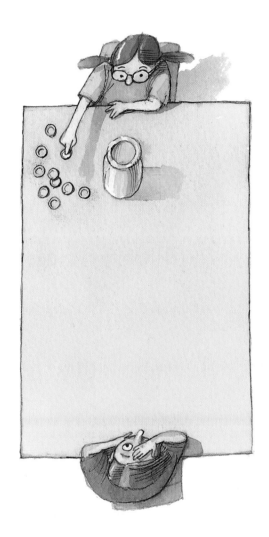

2. Ask the person to direct you ("to the right, now forward ..."). When he thinks your hand is directly above the jar he should tell you to drop the coin. Does the coin drop into the jar? Try this with each of the coins. How many make it into the jar?

3. Now ask him to put a hand over one eye, and try the same thing again. How many coins make it into the jar this time?

Test more people. Can they judge better with one eye or two?

27

Pete was minding his own business when he started to feel funny. Very funny. He felt like he had ants in his pants. Then under one arm. Then between his toes. Then he felt antsy all over. Oh-oh! Could Danoid be testing his sense of touch?

"Data verified," Danoid said. "The Earthling can feel with all parts of his body. But some parts of the Earthling body are more sensitive than others."

 SCIENCE FAIR IDEA

Which body parts are most sensitive?

Equipment

a blindfold
a paper clip bent into a U like this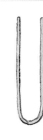

Method

1. Blindfold someone and touch one or both prongs of the paper clip lightly against the back of his hand. Ask him to tell you how many prongs he feels.

2. Test other parts of his body — fingertip, foot, cheek, the middle of his back, tongue, knee and lip. Touch him with one prong sometimes; other times with two. Keep a record of his guesses. Does he guess correctly for some body parts and not for others?

Are some areas more sensitive than others? Test more people to find out.

EARTHDATABANK: Senses

The average Earthling has about 10 000 taste buds. Young Earthlings have more; older Earthlings have fewer.

Touch receptors just under the skin of the Earthling can detect five sensations: contact, pressure, pain, heat and cold. The adult Earthling has about 640 000 of these receptors.

Earthlings can sense four main tastes: sweet, salty, sour and bitter. They are most sensitive to bitter tastes. Many bitter substances are poisonous. Being very sensitive to them can make the difference between life and death. In each nostril, there is a patch of smell receptors about the size of the Earthling thumbnail.

Earthling ears are more than auditory receptors. Balance is also monitored by the inner ear.

The eyes supply about 80 per cent of an Earthling's data about the world.

Report to: The Commander
From: Danoid
Subject: The subject's data receptors

Pinocchio has an unusual data-collection system made up of five parts. There are separate receptors for visual and auditory data. These are called the "eyes" and "ears." The subject also has receptors in the nose and mouth and under the skin. Each part of the system seems to work with the others to give the brain information. The brain analyzes the data and decides what to do.

As a test, Danoid put a cold object, called an ice cube, inside the clothing of Pinocchio. The sensors under the skin immediately flashed a message to the brain, which instructed Pinocchio to get rid of the ice cube by hopping up and down. The response time was impressive.

Danoid peers into Pete's digestive system

Studying always made Pete hungry. The night before a math test, he'd eat everything in the fridge. But he hadn't realized that being studied would make him hungry, too. He turned out his pockets and counted his change.

"So, Danoid, want some fries?"

"Define 'fries,' please."

"Fries. Food. It gives me energy."

"Ah ... fuel. This is Danoid's fuel." A pincer held out a bottle labeled "Odorless, Low-fat, High-fiber, Organic, Vitamin-enriched Fuel."

Pete opened the bottle and poured some pellets into his hand. They smelled a lot like hot chocolate. Pete couldn't resist — he popped a bright green pellet into his mouth. Yechhh! It tasted like a stale cookie with liver filling. He had to eat five fries to get the taste out of his mouth.

"Where did the fuel go?" asked Danoid.

Pete patted his stomach. "It's in here." That gave him an idea. "Hey, why don't I eat some fries while you scan."

The Earthling digestive system

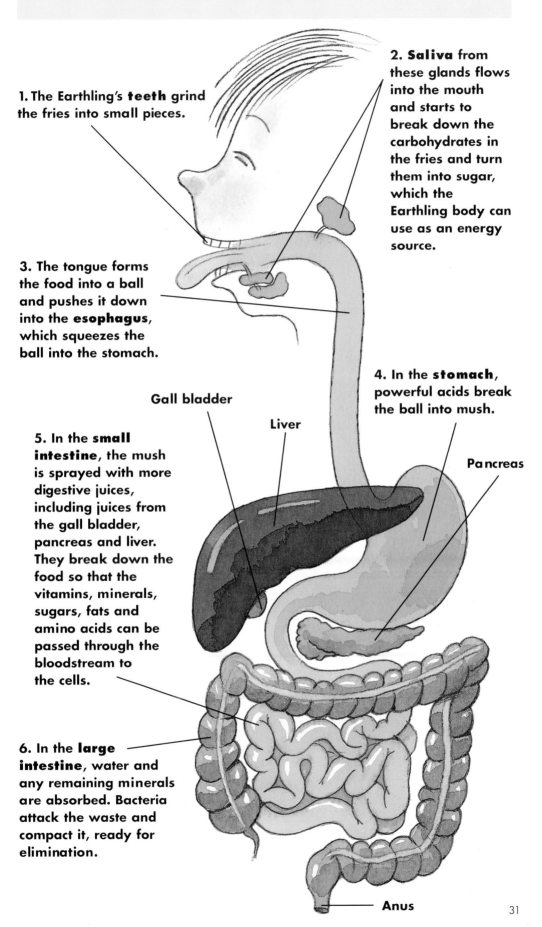

1. The Earthling's **teeth** grind the fries into small pieces.

2. **Saliva** from these glands flows into the mouth and starts to break down the carbohydrates in the fries and turn them into sugar, which the Earthling body can use as an energy source.

3. The tongue forms the food into a ball and pushes it down into the **esophagus**, which squeezes the ball into the stomach.

4. In the **stomach**, powerful acids break the ball into mush.

Gall bladder

Liver

Pancreas

5. In the **small intestine**, the mush is sprayed with more digestive juices, including juices from the gall bladder, pancreas and liver. They break down the food so that the vitamins, minerals, sugars, fats and amino acids can be passed through the bloodstream to the cells.

6. In the **large intestine**, water and any remaining minerals are absorbed. Bacteria attack the waste and compact it, ready for elimination.

Anus

31

Pete had just finished his fries and was licking the salt off his fingers when Danoid asked: "How much energy do you get from food?"

"Depends on what I eat. Some foods have more calories than others."

"What is a calorie?"

"It's a unit of energy, just like a kilogram and a pound are units of weight." Danoid whirred and clicked. Pete tried again. "Everything I eat has calories, and everything I do uses calories."

Danoid whirred some more. "How do you use up the calories you just ate?"

Eat and run

Equipment

a pencil and paper
a calculator

Method

Running uses up about 10 calories per minute. Cycling uses up about 2. Calculate how many minutes you would have to run and cycle to use up the calories from each of the foods.

Food	Number of calories
small cheeseburger	300
hot dog with mustard	280
1-scoop vanilla ice cream cone	250
a slice of cheese pizza	153
a slice of watermelon	118
10 jelly beans	110
a boiled egg	79
a chocolate chip cookie	52
a raw carrot	31
1 french fry	15

"According to EARTHDATABANK, the Earthling digestive system is a tube about 9 m (30 ft.) long. How long does it take food to pass through it?"

Pete had noticed that when he ate corn, it didn't get completely digested. What if he used the corn to time the digestion process?

How long does food take to travel through the digestive system?

Equipment

fresh or frozen corn

Method

1. Have several people eat corn with a meal and note the time the corn was eaten.

2. Ask your subjects to watch for undigested corn when they have a bowel movement. How long does it take for the corn to pass through each person's system?

3. Figure out the average time by adding all the times up and dividing by the number of people.

Saliva glands at the back of the Earthling's mouth produce more than 1 L (1 qt.) of saliva every day.

Over a lifetime, the average Earthling will consume 36 t (40 tn.) of food.

Ask Earthlings where their stomach is and they will probably point to their belt. Actually, the Earthling stomach is higher up, protected by the rib cage.

An adult Earthling's stomach can hold 2 L (2 qt.) of food at one time.

One of the digestive juices in the stomach, hydrochloric acid, is strong enough to strip the paint off a spacecraft.

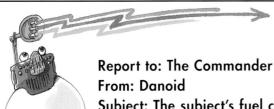

Report to: The Commander
From: Danoid
Subject: The subject's fuel consumption

Pinocchio's body has a hole all the way through it, like a Memoid doughnut. Fuel, called "food," is dropped into the top of the hole (the "mouth") and passes through a series of tubes and pouches. Along the way, the food is mashed and broken down by chemical substances. Energy is extracted and passed along to the cells for growth, repair and movement. The solid leftovers fall out the bottom of the hole (the "anus"). The liquid leftovers exit through another hole.

Pinocchio reports that young Earthlings wear leftover catchers. Older Earthlings go to special rooms to deposit their waste material. Danoid has not seen one of these rooms. Perhaps they are like Memoid banks.

Danoid bones up on Pete's bones

A dog was snuffling around the garbage can at the fish-and-chip stand. Down the beach, someone called, "Here, Fang! Come on, boy," but the dog was playing deaf.

"Fang — that is Danoid's aunt's name." The alien's data receptors swiveled to collect data on the dog. "Why does this Fang have so much hair and walk on four legs?"

"Because… because… he's a dog. They do that." Danoid's questions weren't getting easier.

The alien whirred and clicked like mad. "Danoid will investigate." With that, a blast of light from the data receptors hit the dog, making it look like a walking X-ray.

"Awesome," gasped Pete. Then the blast of light hit him and he could see right through his skin to his bones. "Danoid!" he yelped.

"X-ray vision. Standard feature on this unit. It reveals that the dog has 321 structural units."

"Structural units?" Sometimes Pete wished he had a translator. "You mean bones?" Just then the dog found a steak bone left over from a beach barbecue. "That's a bone." Pete pointed.

"Here, Fang," said Danoid, imitating the call he had heard earlier.

The dog trotted over, dropped the bone and sniffed at Danoid. Then it lifted one leg.

The major bones of the Earthling body

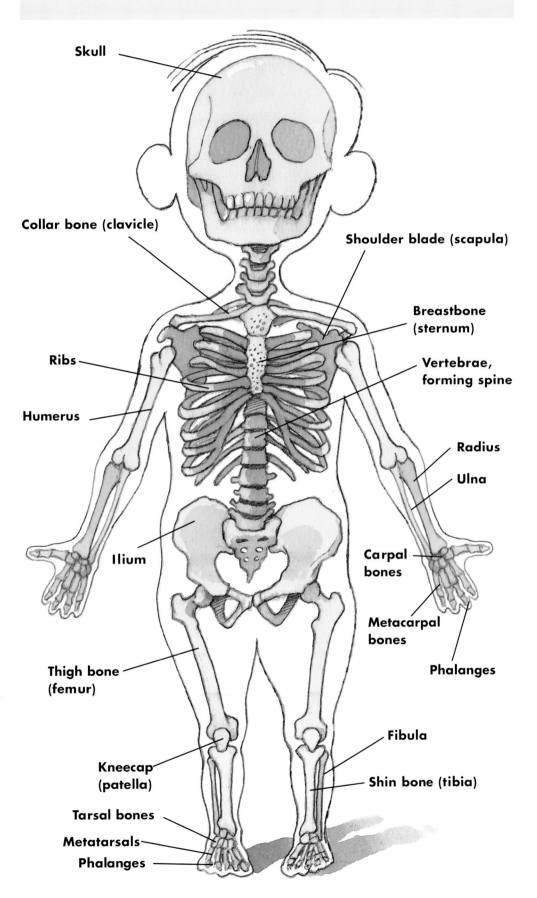

Skull

Collar bone (clavicle)

Shoulder blade (scapula)

Breastbone (sternum)

Ribs

Vertebrae, forming spine

Humerus

Radius

Ulna

Ilium

Carpal bones

Metacarpal bones

Thigh bone (femur)

Phalanges

Fibula

Kneecap (patella)

Shin bone (tibia)

Tarsal bones

Metatarsals

Phalanges

By the time Pete had explained about dogs and fire hydrants and had wiped off Danoid, Fang had run away with the bone. Danoid scanned Pete's forearm.

An Earthling bone

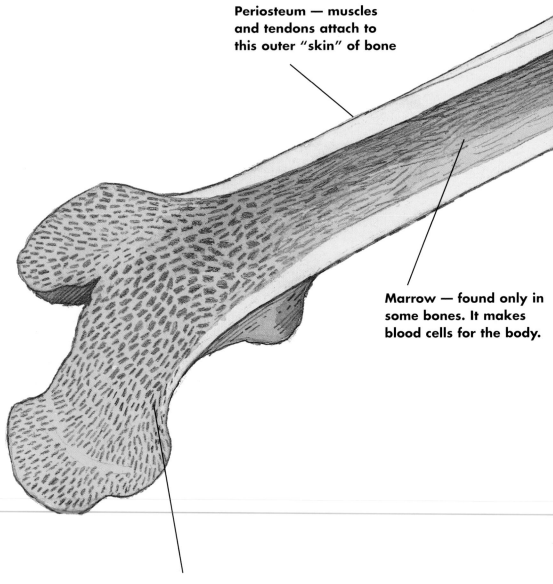

Periosteum — muscles and tendons attach to this outer "skin" of bone

Marrow — found only in some bones. It makes blood cells for the body.

Spongy bone — lighter in weight than solid bone

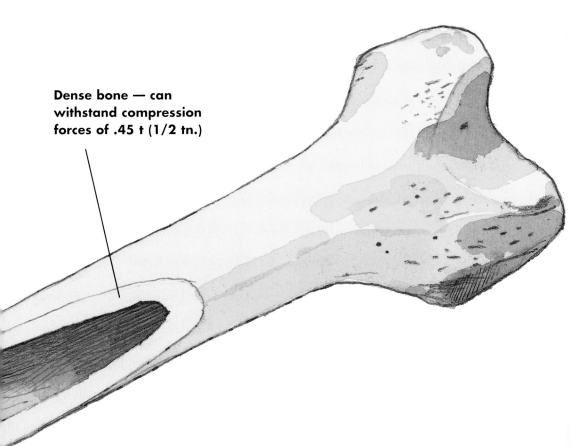

Dense bone — can withstand compression forces of .45 t (1/2 tn.)

EARTHDATABANK: Bones

The number of bones in Earthlings depends on age. At birth they have 350 bones, but some bones (including ones in the head) fuse together. By the time they are adults, they have only 206 bones.

Earthling bones start out soft, like the material at the tip of the nose. This is called cartilage. The bones harden with age.

The bones manufacture new bone material. Every ten years the bones are completely replaced and the Earthling has a whole new skeleton.

Bones are one-third water. The rest is calcium, phosphorus and collagen.

"Are all bones the same?" asked Danoid.
Stumped again!

Are all bones the same?

Equipment

colored pencils
paper
bones from different animals (beef, pork, chicken and fish)
a small saw

Method

1. Draw a cross section of a human bone like the one you see here. Label the parts.

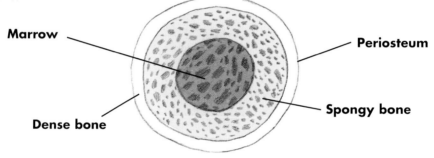

Marrow

Periosteum

Dense bone

Spongy bone

2. Compare the bone you have drawn with the ones you have collected. If the bones are not already cut crossways, ask an adult to saw them in two.

Do all the bones have the same parts?

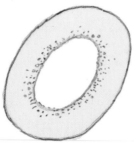

chicken bone

Hey! This chicken bone is hollow. I wonder why.

Report to: The Commander
From: Danoid
Subject: The subject's structural units

Pinocchio does not have a hard outer covering, like Memoids do. Instead, he has an internal structure called a "skeleton" to hold him up. This skeleton is made up of more than 200 separate bones.

The bones are lightweight (about 14 per cent of the subject's weight) but stronger than reinforced concrete, a common Earthling building material.

Bones contain calcium and other minerals. If the subject does not get enough calcium and other minerals from his food, his body will steal them from his bones.

Danoid muscles in on Pete's muscles

Danoid's data receptors were sticking out so far they were almost falling out of their sockets. They were trained on a bodybuilder on the beach. "That Earthling has antennae."

"Those aren't antennae. They're weights."

"Explain 'weights,' please."

"You lift weights to build muscles." Pete made a fist and flexed. A tiny bump appeared on his upper arm. "That's a muscle. We've got them all over our bodies."

Danoid whirred and clicked, a sure sign the alien was thinking. "Where are your weights?"

"I don't have any. You have to buy them."

Danoid bounced and jiggled. "Aha! So Earthlings *do* purchase body parts, like we do on Memo. Do you buy muscles too?"

Sometimes Pete felt as if he were talking to an alien from outer space. Then he remembered: he was. "Our muscles are part of our bodies. We don't buy any body parts." Then Pete thought of artificial limbs and pacemakers and hearing aids. Better not get into that. "We can't just stick stuff on."

"Pity." Danoid's attention turned back to Pete's arm. "What do your muscles do?"

"They let me move — they're attached to my bones."

Pete's smile faded as Danoid's X-ray made him see-through. Oh no, not again!

The major skeletal muscles of the Earthling body

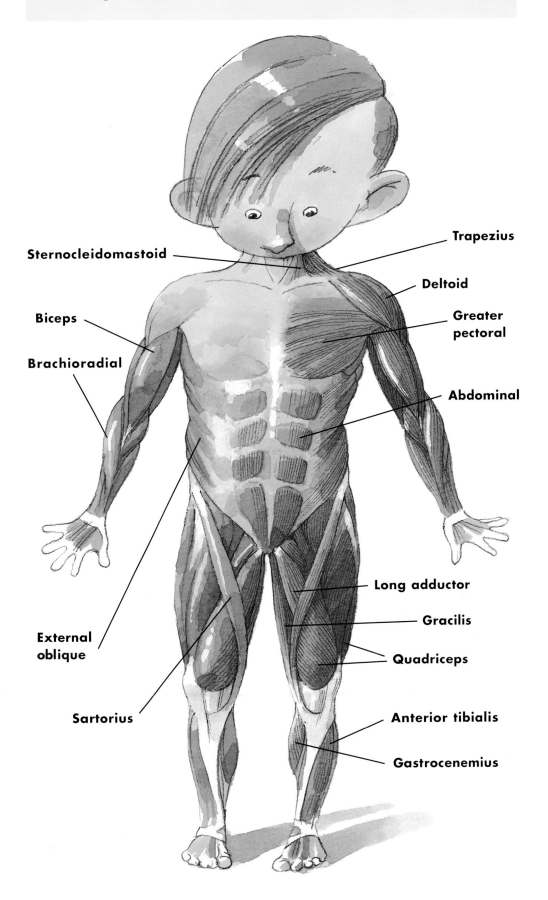

Sternocleidomastoid

Trapezius

Deltoid

Biceps

Greater pectoral

Brachioradial

Abdominal

External oblique

Long adductor

Gracilis

Quadriceps

Sartorius

Anterior tibialis

Gastrocenemius

Danoid was scanning Pete's arm. "Move your muscles, please."
Pete flexed his arm, hand to shoulder, hand to shoulder.
"Curious," said Danoid. "Earthling muscles can only pull."

"Huh?" Pete looked at his arm.

Danoid continued scanning. "To bend your arm, the muscles on one side pull. The muscles on the other side relax. Now push."

Pete pushed against Danoid and watched his muscles being scanned. Danoid was right. Even when he pushed, his muscles only pulled or relaxed.

SCIENCE FAIR IDEA

How do muscles work?

Equipment

4 to 8 people
a string for every person, each about 1 m (3 ft.) long
a small, thick rubber band
plastic containers of various sizes and paper cups

Method

1. Tie the strings around the rubber band as shown.

2. Set the containers on the floor, tipped over on their sides.

3. Have each person hold on to the loose end of a string.

4. By pulling on the strings or relaxing them, work together to put the rubber band over one container and turn it upside down. Now try lifting another container on top of the first. Keep lifting and stacking. You and your friends are acting like teams of muscles, pulling and relaxing to stack the containers.

EARTHDATABANK: Muscles

An Earthling must move about 17 muscles to smile, 72 to say a word and about 200 to take a single step.

As muscles work, lactic acid builds up in them. Too much lactic acid makes muscles feel sore.

The largest muscle in the Earthling body is the one they sit on. The smallest muscle is the one that moves the stirrup, a tiny bone in the inner ear.

Report to: The Commander
From: Danoid
Subject: The subject's movement facilitators

Pinocchio's skeleton is like a Memoid puppet. The muscles are like the strings. Each muscle can only pull. But working together, pairs or groups of muscles can push, lift and turn the bones.

Earthlings are muscle-bound. The subject has about 650 muscles — almost half his weight. Some Earthlings try to increase the size of their muscles by "working out with weights."

When Pinocchio becomes cold, his muscles quickly contract and relax over and over. The muscle movement generates heat. Pinocchio calls this "shivering."

Danoid gets to the heart of Pete

"Hey, it's the pea brain."

Pete's heart started to pound. Oh no! Brendan the Bully!

"Whazzat?" asked Brendan, ogling Danoid.

Pete's heart was beating so loudly he was sure Brendan could hear it. He said the first thing that came into his head. "It's a ... a ... radio."

"Weird-lookin' radio." Brendan twisted one of Danoid's knobs.

Pete's heart stopped. Then he heard a buttery deejay voice. "Hip hop. We're playing fifties faves all weekend long, so don't go away. And here's the man himself, singing 'Tutti Frutti.'" The sound was coming from Danoid! Pete's heart started beating again. He quickly twisted Danoid's knob and the "radio" fell silent.

"Cool. I'm gonna borrow this thing, pea brain." Brendan put his arms around Danoid. His muscles rippled, he grimaced, sweat broke out, veins bulged ... and nothing happened. Brendan tried again, grunting and groaning with the strain. Danoid didn't budge.

"Ah, man, forget it," he snarled. "This piece of junk's not worth the sweat." He pushed past Pete and strutted off down the boardwalk.

Phew! Usually Brendan beat up anyone in his path. Pete's heart was beating so fast he didn't notice Danoid scanning his chest.

An image of a pumping heart appeared on Danoid's shiny surface.

The Earthling heart

The heart is a pump that moves blood around the body. Oxygen-poor blood flows into the right atrium and down into the right ventricle. From there it is pumped to the lungs where it picks up more oxygen. Oxygen-rich blood moves from the lungs into the left atrium and down into the left ventricle. Then it is pumped to the cells of the body.

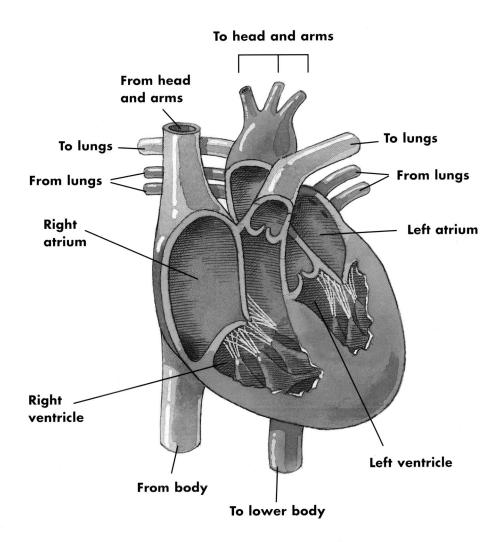

To head and arms

From head and arms

To lungs

To lungs

From lungs

From lungs

Right atrium

Left atrium

Right ventricle

Left ventricle

From body

To lower body

Is that my heart? It's only as big as my fist!

Pete peered at the scan of his heart. He was surprised how small it was — about the size of his clenched fist.

"Do Earthling hearts always pump that fast?" Danoid asked.

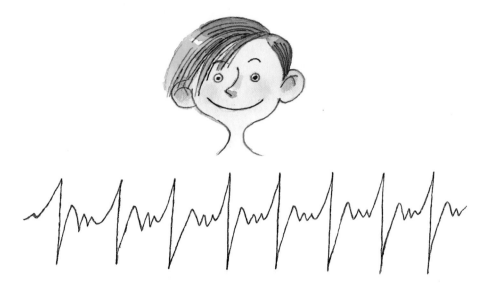

"Nope. It depends on what's happening. If I need more oxygen — say, to run — it pumps faster." Or when I'm about to be pulverized by Brendan, thought Pete. Just the thought of Brendan made his heart pump faster. Hmmm ... could there be a science fair project here?

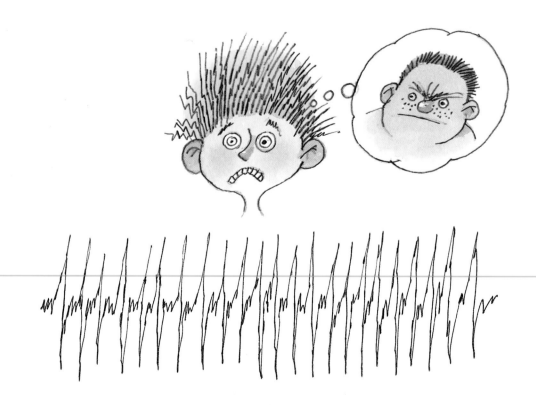

How do moving and emotions affect heart rate?

Equipment

a ball of modeling clay slightly bigger than a pea
a match or toothpick
a watch or clock that shows seconds
a pencil and paper
a very scary video

Method

1. Locate the pulse on the inside of someone's wrist.

2. Press the modeling clay exactly where you felt the pulse. Flatten it slightly to make it stick to the skin.

3. Gently stick one end of a match or toothpick into the modeling clay.

4. Have the person rest her wrist on a table, with the modeling clay up, and make a fist. Watch the match or toothpick move with each pulse. If you can't see it move, press the modeling clay gently against the pulse point.

5. Use the clock to find out how many times her heart beats in a minute.

6. Have her walk around the room several times, then count and record the heartbeats in a minute. Have her walk up and down a flight of stairs twice. Record the heartbeats. Have her run up and down stairs and record the beats. Show her the scariest part of the video. Record her heartbeats now.

Does the heart rate change with each activity? Does fear make the heart speed up?

The Earthling heart beats more than 30 million times a year, 2.5 billion times in an average lifetime.

Earthling blood is bright red or dark red, depending on how much oxygen it is carrying. Bright red blood has lots of oxygen; dark red has very little. (To see dark blood, look at the veins in an Earthling's wrists. It looks almost blue through the skin. As soon as this dark blood is exposed to oxygen, it turns bright red.)

The heart is the strongest muscle in the Earthling body.

Blood is pumped around the body through a system of veins, arteries, arterioles and capillaries. Stretched end to end, this system of blood vessels would measure 96 500 km (60 000 mi.).

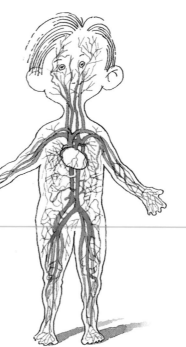

Report to: The Commander
From: Danoid
Subject: The subject's blood-pumping system

Pinocchio's heart is the pump that circulates blood to all parts of the body. The blood carries oxygen, taken in by the lungs, to the cells. It also takes waste gases away from the cells to be expelled through the lungs. This network of heart, lungs and blood vessels is called the "cardiopulmonary system."

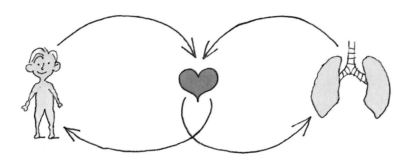

Any action in the body brings more blood rushing to it. Digesting a meal brings more blood to the stomach. Moving a limb brings more blood to that limb. Fear brings more blood to the legs and arms so that the Earthling is ready to fight or run away. That is why Pinocchio's heart pounded when the fat Earthling with the spiked hair appeared.

Danoid monitors Pete's breathing

Pete had been probed and scanned and X-rayed. He had found out that his hair was dead, his heart was the size of his fist, and he had fewer bones than a dog. He had even offered to share his french fries with an alien. Now he'd had enough. Unfortunately, Danoid hadn't.

"Please move rapidly to test the operation of your multidirectional movement facilitators."

"Huh? You mean run? Forget it. I'm walking. Home." Then he remembered his deal with Danoid. "On second thought, what about a ride home in your spacecraft?"

"Run, then ride," said Danoid.

Pete was fed up, but he wasn't going to blow his chance of riding in a spacecraft. So he hitched up his shorts and took off. He ran halfway down the beach and back again.

"Keep running," said Danoid. Pete ran all the way down to the other end of the beach and back. "Repeat, please." Pete did the circuit one more time and collapsed at Danoid's feet. He was puffing and panting.

"What are you doing?" Danoid asked.

"Trying ... to catch ... my breath," gasped Pete.

"What is breath and how do you catch it?"

"Breath. Air. I need the oxygen in air when I run. And after I run. Actually, I need oxygen all the time."

"Catch a breath and let me see." Pete did, and Danoid started scanning Pete's lungs.

Earthling lungs

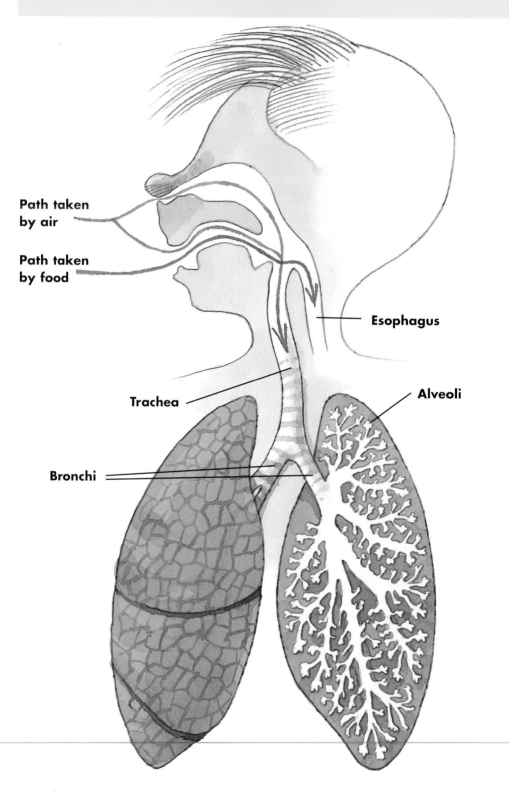

Path taken by air

Path taken by food

Esophagus

Alveoli

Trachea

Bronchi

Air taken in through the respiratory passages (mouth and nose) flows through the trachea and two bronchi into the lungs. There, in tiny sacs called alveoli, an exchange of gases takes place. Oxygen is taken from the air and passed to the blood. Waste carbon dioxide is taken from the blood and passed back into the lungs to be exhaled.

Danoid stopped scanning. "We Memoids do not need air."
"You mean there's no air in your spacecraft?"
"Correct."
"Uh-oh."

Pete's chance of riding in Danoid's spacecraft was disappearing into thin air.
"I need to breathe, Danoid. I need air."

"How much air?"

"How long will the trip to my house take? I can walk it in half an hour."

Danoid chugged away doing a calculation. "Using the most direct vector,
ETA will be about four minutes."

"Hmmmmm...how much air will I need for four minutes?"

How much air do you breathe?

Equipment

a clean, empty 4-L (1-gal.) plastic jug with lid
a bendable plastic drinking straw for each person you test
a measuring cup

Method

1. Half fill a sink with water.

2. Fill the jug with water, right to the top. Screw on the lid. Turn the jug upside down and put its mouth into the water in the sink. Unscrew the lid. If there are any air bubbles in the jug, start again.

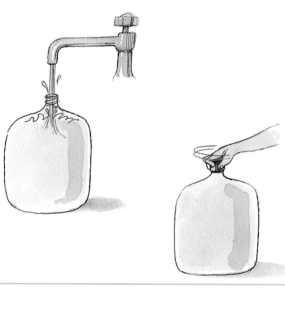

3. Bend up the end of the drinking straw and put it into the mouth of the jug.

4. Have someone hold the jug. Take a deep breath and blow as much air as possible through the straw into the jug. The air will push some of the water out of the jug.

5. Screw on the lid and turn the jug upright again.

6. To see how much air you breathed out, fill the jug up with water using the measuring cup. The amount of water you add is the amount of air in one breath.

If I count the number of breaths I take in four minutes and multiply by the air in one breath, that's how much air I'll need to get home.

EARTHDATABANK : Lungs

Earthlings filter dust and dirt out of the air before it reaches their lungs. Hairs and mucus in the nose trap stuff and move it into the back of the nose and then into the throat, where it is swallowed. Sometimes dirt and dust are expelled out the nose in a explosion of air. This is called a sneeze. Warning to Memoids: Droplets from a sneeze may travel as fast as an Earthling car on the highway and land up to 3.7 m (12 ft.) away.

Smaller Earthlings breathe faster than large ones because their lungs are smaller and cannot extract as much oxygen.

The lungs are part of Pinocchio's cardiopulmonary system. In the lungs, blood pumped by the heart continually unloads carbon dioxide, a waste gas, and takes on oxygen. The lungs push the waste gas out of the body into the environment and pull outside oxygen into the body.

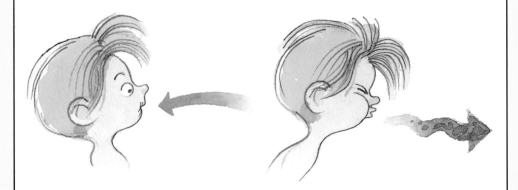

Without a steady supply of oxygen, Pinocchio claims he would become inoperational. He says that, even when he tries to, he cannot stop breathing for long. It seems that the Earthling brain monitors carbon dioxide in the blood. If the level of carbon dioxide gets too high, the brain signals the body to breathe.

TIME TO RETURN TO BASE, DANOID

Last encounter

The next few weeks were a bit of a blur to Pete.

Danoid had given him a ride home in the spacecraft, which was a bit like riding in a very fast sideways elevator. They had shaken hands — Pete's hand, Danoid's data receptor — and Pete had finally explained to Danoid that he was Pete and that Pinocchio was, well, Pinocchio. The last Pete saw of Danoid was a data receptor waving as the spacecraft rose vertically into the sky. He would miss the little guy.

Pete had been stashing the scuba tank in the garage when the TV news truck squealed to a halt in front of the house. A videocam made right for him, with some greasy guy in hot pursuit, yelling, "Kid, kid — didja see it?" The newspaper reporters weren't far behind. Then the networks got involved. And the police. And something called the Institute for the Study of Extraterrestrial Life. It was a zoo. But all Pete would say was that he'd seen a red disk climbing in the western sky. Probably a Frisbee.

Still, Pete became a local celebrity for a while. Even Brendan stopped bullying him. And, using what he and Danoid had learned about the human body, Pete won first place in the science fair. Can you guess which project he chose?

Danoid locked on to a radio beam from a communications satellite and heard about the sighting of an alien spacecraft on Earth. "Another close encounter," said the Commander.
"I'll miss the big guy," sighed Danoid.
Then the alien analyzed the data on the Earthling...

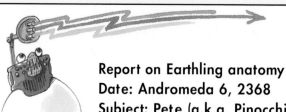

Report on Earthling anatomy
Date: Andromeda 6, 2368
Subject: Pete (a.k.a. Pinocchio)
Submitted by: Danoid of Planet Memo

The subject called Pete willingly cooperated in a series of tests on the Earthling anatomy. Danoid respectfully submits these findings:

• Earthlings come in a variety of ages, counted in "years." The subject became operational 11 years ago. He has not had any new body parts since then. His original parts have grown with him.

• Although they have the same body parts (planet connectors, manipulatives, etc.), each Earthling looks different.

• Every part of the Earthling body has a function. There are no add-on decorative accessories, as on Memo.

• Many of the body parts work with other parts to form systems — for example, the digestive system and the cardiopulmonary system.

• Earthlings use food and oxygen from the air to produce energy to grow, move and even repair themselves. This saves on the costly repairs common on Memo. For serious body work, Earthlings are taken into specialized facilities called "hospitals."

• The Earthling Pete was good-humored and curious. It is not known whether all Earthlings share these characteristics.

Signed,

Danoid

Index